BE PRESENT.

CHOOSE WELL.

REPEAT.

A Grounded Philosophy for
Peace, Purpose & Performance

By Dan Armida

First Edition

Published by: Be Present Press

ISBN (Paperback): 979-8-9950301-0-2

ISBN (Hardcover): 979-8-9950301-7-1

Printed in the United States of America

For my Family

For your unconditional love, support and belief

And for those who are doing their best in

moments that don't feel their best

FULL CHAPTER OVERVIEW

PART I — THE OUTCOME TRAP

Chapter 1 - When Performance Becomes Identity

How worth quietly becomes tied to results and why it costs peace.

Chapter 2 - The Illusion of Pressure

Why pressure isn't in the moment, but in the meaning, we assign to it.

Chapter 3 - Why Confidence Disappears When You Need It Most

How attachment collapses confidence and what stabilizes it.

PART II — THE OPERATING SYSTEM

Chapter 4 - Presence Is Power

Why attention, not control, is the real source of strength.

Chapter 5 - You Always Have a Choice

How agency lives in the smallest moments.

Chapter 6 - Letting Go Without Letting Up

How to care deeply without carrying the weight.

HOW TO USE THIS BOOK

This is not a book to rush.

Read it slowly.
Pause when something lands.
Return to sections when life gets heavy.

You don't need to "agree" with everything immediately.
You only need to notice what resonates.

The goal is not perfection.

The goal is return.

CHAPTER 1

When Performance Becomes Identity

Chapter Mantra
My worth is not decided by today's result.

Most people don't wake up one day and decide to tie their self-worth to performance. It happens gradually.

Praise when you succeed.
Silence when you don't.
Belonging when you're "on."
Distance when you're not.

<u>Over time, a quiet equation forms:</u>

When I perform well, I feel valuable.
When I don't, something feels wrong.

This equation is rarely spoken out loud, but it governs behavior.

The Invisible Contract

<u>Many people live by an invisible contract that says:</u>

I'm allowed to feel confident when things go well

I'm allowed to feel proud when I succeed

I'm allowed to feel at peace once I earn it

The problem isn't effort.

The problem is postponing peace.

<u>When identity is tied to outcomes:</u>

confidence becomes fragile

fear increases in important moments

comparison becomes automatic

joy becomes conditional

You can be talented, prepared and committed, but still feel constantly on edge.

Why Big Moments Feel Heavy

<u>When a moment "matters," what's really happening is this:</u>

The mind believes something is at stake, not just the outcome, but you.

That's why hands tighten.
That's why decisions slow.
That's why confidence disappears when you want it most.

Not because you're unprepared, because the moment feels like a verdict.

And no one performs freely when they feel judged.

A Different Starting Point

<u>This book begins with a different assumption:</u>

You are already enough.

Not as a slogan.
As a foundation.

Enough doesn't mean finished.
Enough doesn't mean complacent.
Enough means your worth is not on trial.

<u>From that place:</u>

effort becomes cleaner

feedback becomes useful

mistakes become information

Reflection

Notice where you try to earn peace.

Notice when confidence rises and falls with results.

Not to judge, just to see.

Awareness is always the first step toward freedom.

Chapter Reflection Thought
When results define how I see myself, effort becomes heavy and moments feel like judgments rather than opportunities.

Chapter 1 Reflection

When Performance Becomes Identity

1. What stood out to me most in this chapter?

2. Where do I notice my sense of worth rising or falling with results right now?

3. What would change if I separated who I am from how I perform this week?

Key Takeaway (in my own words):

Coach's Pause:
If I were reminding myself of one truth when results feel heavy, what would it be?

CHAPTER 2

The Illusion of Pressure

Chapter Mantra
The moment is neutral; I choose the meaning.

We talk about pressure as if it's something real.

Pressure moments.
Pressure situations.
Performing under pressure.

But the court doesn't change.
The field doesn't change.
The task doesn't change.

So where does pressure come from?

Pressure Is Meaning, Not a Moment

Pressure appears when the mind decides:

this matters more than usual

this says something about me

this outcome carries extra weight

Pressure is not created by the situation.

It's created by meaning.

And that changes everything.

Because if pressure were inherent to the moment, you'd be powerless.

But if pressure is created internally, choice still exists.

Why Pressure Feels Physical

The body responds to perceived threat, not reality.

<u>When identity feels at risk:</u>

heart rate increases

muscles tighten

attention narrows

This isn't weakness.
It's biology.

The issue isn't that the response happens.

It's what we do next.

Reframing the Moment

There are no pressure moments.

There are only moments asking for a response.

When you remove the belief that the moment defines you, it becomes workable again.

Reflection

<u>Next time you feel pressure, ask:</u>

What meaning am I giving this moment?

What am I afraid it says about me?

What response is actually required right now?

Then return:

Be Present. Choose Well. Repeat.

Chapter Reflection Thought
Pressure is rarely in the situation itself, it's in the story I attach to what the moment says about me.

Chapter 2 Reflection

The Illusion of Pressure

1. What stood out to me most in this chapter?

2. What situations in my life feel "pressure-filled," and what meaning am I giving them?

3. How could I approach one upcoming moment with less added meaning?

Key Takeaway (in my own words):

Coach's Pause:
When I feel pressure, what reminder helps bring me back to the moment?

CHAPTER 3

Why Confidence Disappears
When You Need It Most

Chapter Mantra
Confidence returns when identity is no longer on trial.

Confidence doesn't disappear.

It gets covered.

And what covers it is not fear or lack of preparation.

It's attachment.

Fragile Confidence

Confidence built on outcomes feels strong, until uncertainty enters. Then it tightens.

Because it was never built to survive the weight of needing an outcome.

When Confidence Switches Jobs

In high-stakes moments, confidence often stops supporting expression and starts guarding the ego.

You play safe.
You hesitate.
You protect yourself.

Not because you don't believe, but because belief feels risky.

Stable Confidence

The strongest confidence comes from certainty of self,
not certainty of success.

I'll be okay regardless of outcome

This moment doesn't define me

I can live with my response

That confidence is quiet.
Available.
Durable.

Reflection

<u>When confidence feels shaky, ask:</u>

What am I afraid this moment says about me?

What would change if I released that meaning?

What's the next aligned action?

Then choose.

Chapter Reflection Thought
The more I need an outcome to validate me, the less freely I am able to act within the moment.

Chapter 3 Reflection

Why Confidence Disappears When You Need It Most

1. What stood out to me most in this chapter?

2. When does my confidence feel most fragile, and what am I attached to in those moments?

3. What would it look like to trust myself without needing certainty of success?

Key Takeaway (in my own words):

Coach's Pause:
What helps me return to steady confidence when doubt shows up?

CHAPTER 4

Presence Is Power

Chapter Mantra
Power lives in where my attention is.

Presence is often misunderstood as calm, quiet or passive.

But presence is not passive at all.

Presence is engaged awareness.

Presence is strength without force.

Presence is where power actually lives.

Where Power Is Usually Lost

When moments feel hard, attention rarely stays where it belongs.

It moves:

into the future (What if this goes wrong?)

into the past (Why did I mess that up?)

into comparison (What will they think?)

And when attention leaves the present moment, power goes with it.

You cannot respond well to a moment you are not fully in.

The Present Moment Is the Only Place You Can Choose

You cannot choose in the past.
You cannot choose in the future.

Choice only exists now.

That's why presence is not a mindset trick, it's a prerequisite for agency, choice and control.

When you are present:

response becomes available

clarity increases

emotion softens

effort becomes cleaner

Not because things feel easy, but because nothing extra
is being carried.

Presence Is Not the Absence of Thought

<u>Presence does not mean:</u>

no thoughts

no emotion

no nerves

Presence allows all of that.

It simply refuses to let any of it take over the steering
wheel.

You don't eliminate experience.
You stay with it.

Why Presence Feels Rare

Presence requires honesty.

<u>It asks you to stop:</u>

rehearsing outcomes

narrating your performance

judging yourself mid-moment

Many people stay busy mentally because stillness feels vulnerable.

But what we avoid feeling doesn't disappear.
It shows up louder later.

Presence as Courage

Presence is not comfort. It's courage.

<u>The courage to stay with:</u>

uncertainty

effort

discomfort

incomplete information

<u>Presence says:</u>
I don't need certainty to act.
I don't need guarantees to engage.
I don't need outcomes to be okay.

That is real power.

Reflection

When you notice yourself leaving the moment:

return to the breath

return to the body

return to the task

The return is the practice.

Chapter Reflection Thought
When my attention leaves the present moment, my ability to respond with clarity and intention leaves with it. When you return to the present, you return to choice.

Chapter 4 Reflection

Presence Is Power

1. What stood out to me most in this chapter?

2. Where does my attention tend to go when things get uncomfortable?

3. How can I practice returning to the present moment more intentionally this week?

Key Takeaway (in my own words):

Coach's Pause:
What simple cue helps me come back to now when my mind drifts?

CHAPTER 5

You Always Have a Choice

Chapter Mantra
I may not choose the moment, but I choose my response.

You always have a choice.

There are moments when it doesn't feel that way.

Moments when emotion rises fast.
Moments when reaction feels automatic.
Moments when circumstances feel unfair.

In those moments, choice can feel like a luxury.

It isn't.

It's a skill.

Choice Does Not Mean Control

Choice does not mean controlling:

outcomes

emotions

situations

other people

You don't always get to choose what happens or how you feel.

But you always get to choose how you respond to what's here.

That choice may be small.
It may be quiet.
It may last only a second.

But it exists.

Reaction vs. Response

Reaction is automatic.
Response is intentional.

Reaction happens when emotion takes the wheel.
Response happens when awareness creates space.

Response does not mean slow.
It means conscious.

The Space Where Freedom Lives

Between stimulus and action, there is a space.

That space might be brief, but it's real.

Inside it lives:

responsibility

integrity

agency

freedom

The moment you notice that space, you reclaim choice.

Choosing Well Is Not Choosing Perfectly

<u>Choosing well does not mean:</u>

always making the right decision

never making mistakes

never feeling regret

<u>Choosing well means:</u>

acting in alignment with values

choosing effort over avoidance

choosing honesty over image

You can choose well and still lose. And still walk away whole.

Reflection

<u>When overwhelmed, ask:</u>

What choice is available right now?

What response would I respect later?

Then choose that.

Chapter Reflection Thought
Freedom does not come from controlling circumstances, it comes from recognizing choice where I once believed there was none. Choice creates freedom. Freedom allows effort without fear.

Chapter 5 Reflection

You Always Have a Choice

1. What stood out to me most in this chapter?

2. Where in my life do I forget that choice is still available?

3. What response would I feel proud of choosing in a challenging moment this week?

Key Takeaway (in my own words):

Coach's Pause:
When I feel stuck, what question helps me remember my agency?

CHAPTER 6

Letting Go Without
Letting Up

Chapter Mantra
I give full effort without carrying the weight.

One of the biggest fears people have about "letting go" is:

If I let go, I won't care.
If I let go, I'll lose my edge.

That fear makes sense.

But it's based on a misunderstanding.

Letting Go Is Not Quitting

Letting go does not mean:

lowering standards

reducing effort

becoming passive

Letting go means releasing what was never yours to control:

outcomes

opinions

judgments

future guarantees

You don't let go of effort.
You let go of attachment.

High Effort, Low Weight

<u>The strongest performers live here:</u>

High effort.
Low attachment.

They prepare fully.
They show up completely.
They compete intensely.

But they don't carry the moment home with them.

That's not weakness.

That's freedom.

Caring vs. Carrying

You can care deeply without carrying the weight.

<u>Caring fuels:</u>

preparation

focus

commitment

<u>Carrying creates:</u>

tension

fear

over-control

One helps performance.
One hurts it.

Letting Go Makes You Better

<u>When you stop carrying outcomes:</u>

attention sharpens

decisions simplify

recovery improves

joy returns

Letting go doesn't make you careless.

It makes you present.

Reflection

<u>After any performance, ask:</u>

What can I learn?

What can I release?

What's the next honest step?

Keep the lesson.
Release the weight.

Chapter Reflection Thought
I can care deeply, prepare fully, and still release the burden of needing things to go a certain way. When you stop proving, you can finally be.

Chapter 6 Reflection

Letting Go Without Letting Up

1. What stood out to me most in this chapter?

2. Where do I notice myself carrying more than I need to right now?

3. What would full effort without added weight look like for me this week?

Key Takeaway (in my own words):

Coach's Pause:
If I were coaching myself through this chapter, what reminder would I offer when things feel heavy?

CHAPTER 7

You Are Enough,
Before The Results

Chapter Mantra
I start from enough, not from proving.

You are enough, before the results.

This sentence is hard to believe for many people.

Not because it isn't true,
but because of what they were taught instead.

Worth is earned.
Peace comes later.
Confidence is conditional.

So, we strive not just to grow, but to prove.

The Quiet Agreement

Many people live by this unspoken agreement:

Once I achieve enough, I'll feel worthy.
Once I prove myself, I'll relax.

The problem is the finish line keeps moving.

Enough Does Not Mean Done

Enough does not mean:

finished

complacent

lacking ambition

<u>Enough means:</u>

your worth is not on trial

effort is a choice, not a plea

growth is desire-driven, not fear-driven

When you start from enough, you don't stop striving.

You stop proving.

Why This Changes Everything

<u>When identity is stable:</u>

feedback becomes useful

mistakes become information

comparison loses power

joy returns to the journey

Pressure softens because nothing essential is at risk.

Reflection

<u>When you notice yourself chasing worth, ask:</u>

What am I trying to earn right now?

What would change if I believed I was already enough?

What choice would I make from that place?

Then choose from there.

Chapter Reflection Thought
When worth no longer needs to be earned, effort becomes an expression of growth rather than a plea for validation.

Chapter 7 Reflection

You Are Enough, Before The Results

1. What stood out to me most in this chapter?

2. In what ways do I still try to earn worth or peace through achievement?

3. How would I approach my goals differently if I truly started from enough?

Key Takeaway (in my own words):

Coach's Pause:
What truth do I need to remember when I start proving instead of being?

CHAPTER 8

The Internal Scoreboard

Chapter Mantra
I measure what I can control.

Most people live by a scoreboard they didn't choose.

Wins and losses.

Stats and rankings.

Approval and criticism.

Likes, praise, playing time, titles.

The external scoreboard is loud, public and constantly updating.

The problem isn't that it exists.

The problem is when it becomes the only measure.

Living on the External Scoreboard

<u>When success is measured externally:</u>

confidence rises and falls daily

comparison becomes automatic

motivation becomes emotional

peace depends on performance

<u>You're always checking:</u>

How did I do?

How do I look?

Where do I stand?

That way of living creates urgency but not fulfillment.

The Cost of Comparison

Comparison quietly drains joy.

It turns teammates into benchmarks.
It turns growth into a race.
It turns effort into evaluation.

Comparison doesn't tell you who you are.

It tells you who you aren't, in that moment.

Choosing a Different Scoreboard

<u>An internal scoreboard measures:</u>

effort

alignment

integrity

response

growth

<u>It asks different questions:</u>

Did I show up honestly?

Did I respond well under stress?

Did I live my standards today?

These are things you can answer, regardless of outcome.

Why the Internal Scoreboard Stabilizes Confidence

<u>When you live by internal standards:</u>

confidence becomes steadier

feedback becomes useful

mistakes lose their sting

success becomes enjoyable, not stressful

You stop outsourcing your self-worth.

Not because you don't care,
but because you care about the right things.

Results Still Matter, Just Not First

The internal scoreboard doesn't replace results.

It organizes them.

Results become information.
Feedback becomes guidance.
Wins become moments, not identities.

Reflection

<u>At the end of each day, ask:</u>

Did I live by my standards today?

Where did I respond well?

Where can I choose better tomorrow?

Reflect. Don't judge.

Chapter Reflection Thought
The standards I choose to live by quietly shape my confidence, my peace, and the way I experience success. Standards don't eliminate emotion; they prevent emotion from controlling behavior.

Chapter 8 Reflection

The Internal Scoreboard

1. What stood out to me most in this chapter?

2. What external measures do I rely on most to evaluate myself?

3. What internal standard do I want to prioritize this week instead?

Key Takeaway (in my own words):

Coach's Pause:
When comparison shows up, what helps me return to my standards?

CHAPTER 9

Responding Well
When It's Hard

Chapter Mantra
The moment after matters most.

Most people don't struggle because things are hard.

They struggle because when things get hard, they lose themselves.

Emotion spikes.
Thoughts race.
The moment tightens.

This chapter is about staying aligned even when the inevitable discomfort shows up.

Difficulty Is Not the Enemy

Hard moments are not mistakes.

They are not interruptions to the process.

They are the process.

<u>Discomfort appears when:</u>

something matters

effort is required

growth is happening

Remove difficulty, and depth disappears.

What Actually Happens Under Stress

When stress hits, the nervous system reacts
automatically.

Attention narrows.
Emotion intensifies.
Old habits surface.

This isn't weakness. It's biology.

The challenge isn't stopping the response.

The challenge is what you do next.

The Moment That Matters Most

<u>The most important moment is not:</u>

the mistake

the setback

the emotion

It's the moment after.

<u>That moment determines whether:</u>

the situation escalates or settles

identity tightens or stays open

growth occurs or stalls

Responding well doesn't mean responding perfectly.

It means responding intentionally.

Emotional Strength Is Behavioral Stability

Emotional strength is not calm feelings.

It's stable behavior during emotional waves.

You don't need fear to disappear.

You need presence. You need choice. You need standards.

Reflection: The Four-Step Reset

<u>When things get hard:</u>

1 - Notice what's happening

2 - Name the emotion

3 - Pause, even briefly, and breathe

4 - Choose the next aligned action

That's it.

Simple. Repeatable. Powerful.

Chapter Reflection Thought
Growth is rarely decided by what goes wrong, but by how I respond in the moments immediately after. You don't need to feel ready to move forward. You need to move to become ready.

Chapter 9 Reflection

Responding Well When It's Hard

1. What stood out to me most in this chapter?

2. How do I typically respond in the moments immediately after things go wrong?

3. What would responding well look like for me in those moments?

Key Takeaway (in my own words):

Coach's Pause:
What small reset helps me regain alignment after a setback?

CHAPTER 10

Action Before Feeling

Chapter Mantra
I act aligned, not motivated.

Most people wait.

They wait to feel confident.
They wait to feel motivated.
They wait to feel ready.

While they wait, life keeps moving.

The Myth of Readiness

<u>Many people believe the order is:</u>
Feel confident → take action → succeed.

<u>In reality, it works the opposite way:</u>
Take action → build confidence → learn → repeat.

Waiting to feel ready hands control over to emotion and emotion is inconsistent.

Feelings Inform, They Don't Lead

Feelings fluctuate hourly.

If action depends on feeling:

consistency disappears

discipline weakens

progress stalls

Feelings provide information.
They do not provide instruction.

Action Creates Clarity

<u>Action cuts through:</u>

overthinking

hesitation

imagined outcomes

<u>When you act:</u>

momentum builds

anxiety softens

focus sharpens

Clarity follows movement.

Discipline as Self-Respect

Discipline is not punishment.

Discipline is self-respect in action.

<u>It says:</u>
I will act in alignment with who I want to be regardless
of mood.

Reflection

<u>When stuck, ask:</u>

What is the next small action?

What response would future-me respect?

Then do that.

Not to feel better, but to be aligned.

Chapter Reflection Thought
Clarity and confidence are often the result of action, not the conditions required before it. What you repeat becomes who you trust yourself to be.

Chapter 10 Reflection

Action Before Feeling

1. What stood out to me most in this chapter?

2. Where am I currently waiting to feel ready before taking action?

3. What is one small, aligned action I can take even if I don't feel ready?

Key Takeaway (in my own words):

Coach's Pause:
When hesitation shows up, what helps me move anyway?

CHAPTER 11

Habits That Build Identity

Most people think identity is something you discover.

In reality, it's something you build.

Not through dramatic moments.

Through what you do repeatedly, when no one is watching.

Identity Is Behavior Repeated

Every habit is a vote.

<u>A vote for:</u>

who you are becoming

what you value

how you relate to yourself

One choice doesn't define you.

Patterns do.

Why Habits Matter More Than Motivation

Motivation is emotional.
Habits are structural.

Motivation fades.
Habits remain.

When life gets busy or stressful, habits are what stay in place.

Habits as Anchors

Good habits don't trap you. They anchor you.

<u>They create:</u>

predictability in chaos

alignment during stress

stability when emotions fluctuate

Non-Negotiables

Non-negotiables are small actions you commit to regardless of mood.

They're not extreme.

They're consistent.

<u>Examples:</u>

returning to breath under stress

resetting after mistakes

reflecting at the end of the day

<u>These actions quietly reinforce:</u>
This is who I am.

Reflection

Choose a small set of daily non-negotiables.

Make them realistic.
Make them meaningful.
Return to them often.

Identity forms naturally from repetition.

Chapter Reflection Thought
Small, consistent behaviors quietly shape my identity far more than single moments of intensity ever could.

Chapter 11 Reflection

Habits That Build Identity

1. What stood out to me most in this chapter?

2. What habits currently reinforce the person I am becoming?

3. What small habit would help me live more aligned with who I want to be?

Key Takeaway (in my own words):

Coach's Pause:
What habit, repeated daily, would quietly change everything?

CHAPTER 12

Competing Free

Chapter Mantra
I play to express, not to protect.

Most people believe freedom in performance comes
from confidence.

It doesn't.

Freedom comes from not needing the outcome to go a
certain way in order to be okay.

When that need disappears, something powerful
happens.

You stop bracing.
You stop protecting.
You stop holding back.

And you start competing freely.

What It Means to Compete Free

Competing free does not mean:

being casual

lowering standards

not caring

Competing free means:

full effort

full presence

full engagement

without fear deciding behavior

It is intensity without tension.
Care without weight.
Focus without force.

Why Fear Tightens Performance

Fear doesn't usually say don't try.

<u>It says:</u>

be careful

don't mess this up

protect yourself

That message pulls attention away from the task and toward the self.

You begin performing about the moment instead of in the moment.

<u>Freedom begins when attention returns to:</u>

the body

the breath

the task

the next action

Clean Effort Feels Different

<u>When effort is clean:</u>

movement flows

decisions simplify

recovery is quicker

joy shows up unexpectedly

You're not fighting yourself. You're expressing yourself.

That's why peak performance often feels quiet, not frantic.

Trusting Preparation

Competing free requires trust.

Not blind trust but earned trust.

<u>Trust in:</u>

preparation

habits

your ability to respond

You don't need to replay preparation in the moment. You let it do its job.

Reflection

<u>Before competition, remind yourself:</u>

I don't need this to define me

I trust my preparation

I'm here to respond well

Then return to the task.

Chapter Reflection Thought
When I stop needing the outcome to define me, performance becomes lighter, freer, and more authentic. When you stop needing validation, you start creating influence.

Chapter 12 Reflection

Competing Free

1. What stood out to me most in this chapter?

2. Where do I notice myself protecting instead of expressing?

3. What would it look like to fully express myself without needing the outcome?

Key Takeaway (in my own words):

Coach's Pause:
What helps me trust my preparation and stay free in the moment?

CHAPTER 13

Leadership Is Presence

Chapter Mantra
My steadiness is my leadership.

Leadership is often misunderstood as influence
through voice, authority or control.

But real leadership starts somewhere quieter.

It starts with how you show up when things are

unsettled.

Presence Leads Before Words

Leadership begins before you speak.

<u>It shows up in:</u>

body language

emotional regulation

response to adversity

consistency

People don't look for perfection.

They look for steadiness.

The Power of Emotional Stability

Emotional stability is not suppression.

<u>It's the ability to:</u>

feel emotion

stay aware

choose behavior

<u>When you stay regulated:</u>

decisions improve

conflict de-escalates

trust increases

Your calm becomes a reference point for others.

Leading Without Needing to Be Right

Presence changes how leaders relate to ego.

<u>You don't need to:</u>

win every conversation

defend your image

dominate space

You listen more.
You react less.
You choose your moments.

That restraint builds trust.

Leadership Shows After Mistakes

<u>Leadership is revealed:</u>

after losses

after tension

after disappointment

Not in perfection, but in recovery.

How you reset teaches people what's acceptable.

Reflection

In group settings, ask:

What does this moment need?

What energy am I bringing?

What response would stabilize the room?

Then model it.

Chapter Reflection Thought
People are influenced less by what I say and more by how I show up when things feel uncertain.

Chapter 13 Reflection

Leadership Is Presence

1. What stood out to me most in this chapter?

2. How does my presence affect others when things are uncertain or tense?

3. What kind of energy do I want to model this week?

Key Takeaway (in my own words):

Coach's Pause:
When others look to me, what steadiness do I want them to feel?

CHAPTER 14

When Things Fall Apart

Chapter Mantra
I remain whole when outcomes fall away.

There will be moments when things still fall apart.

A season ends.

A role changes.

An injury happens.

A goal slips away.

No mindset prevents the pain of those moments.

This chapter is about staying whole inside them.

Falling Apart Is Not Failing

When things fall apart, it's easy to believe something went wrong.

But falling apart is not failure.

It's transition.

It's the moment where one chapter ends and the next hasn't formed yet.

When Roles End

Athletes feel this deeply.

When the jersey comes off.
When routine disappears.
When identity feels unclear.

The role was never your value.

It was a place where your values were expressed and values don't end when roles do.

Grief Is Evidence of Care

Grief does not mean weakness.

It means something mattered.

The goal is not to rush through grief.

It's to stay present with it, without letting it define you.

What Remains When Structures Collapse

<u>When outcomes fall away, return to what remains:</u>

presence

choice

integrity

compassion

These don't disappear.

They are portable.

Reflection

<u>When things fall apart, ask:</u>

What is being asked of me right now?

How can I respond with integrity here?

What would kindness toward myself look like today?

Chapter Reflection Thought
*Even when roles, seasons or structures end; my values,
presence and capacity I choose remain.*

Chapter 14 Reflection

When Things Fall Apart

1. What stood out to me most in this chapter?

2. Where am I currently experiencing an ending, change, or uncertainty?

3. How can I remain whole and present in this transition?

Key Takeaway (in my own words):

Coach's Pause:
When life feels unclear, what helps me stay grounded & kind to myself?

CONCLUSION

The Practice That Never Ends

Master Mantra
Be Present. Choose Well. Repeat.

This book was never about mastering pressure or outcomes.

It was about releasing the belief that pressure or outcomes are what defines you.

Along the way, we challenged some familiar ideas:

that confidence must come before action

that worth is earned through outcomes

that peace is a reward for achievement

that struggle means something is wrong

What you've seen is something quieter & far more powerful.

You don't need to eliminate discomfort to live well.
You don't need certainty to move forward.
You don't need outcomes to validate who you are.

You need presence.
You need choice.
You need alignment.

Again and again.

Strength, Redefined

The strongest mindset is not forceful.

It doesn't dominate moments or overpower emotion.
It doesn't rely on intensity, bravado or constant confidence.

The strongest mindset is steady.

It notices what's here.
It chooses how to respond.
It stays aligned even when things are uncomfortable.

It allows life to be honest without turning that honesty into a verdict.

That kind of strength doesn't fade when things get hard.
It shows up because things get hard.

Peace Is Not the Absence of Effort

Peace does not mean disengaging from life.

It means no longer fighting yourself inside it.

<u>When peace becomes the starting point:</u>

effort becomes cleaner

ambition becomes healthier

joy becomes accessible

growth becomes sustainable

You still care deeply.
You still strive.
You still give your best.

You just stop asking outcomes to carry your identity.

The Work Is Simple, Not Easy

The practice you've learned is simple:

Be Present

Choose Well

Repeat

But it's not easy.

You'll forget.
You'll react.
You'll get pulled into old patterns.

That's not failure.

That's life.

The practice isn't perfection.
It's return.

Every time you notice and come back, the mindset strengthens.

What Remains With You

Long after this book is closed, what remains is not information, it's a way of relating to moments:

moments of effort

moments of uncertainty

moments of joy

moments of loss

Those moments will keep coming.

And each time, you'll have a choice.

Not to control the outcome, but to choose who you are in it.

That is where peace lives.
That is where confidence stabilizes.
That is where purpose becomes personal.

One Last Reminder

You don't need to become someone else.

You don't need to prove your worth.

You are already enough and from that place, you get to choose how you live.

Final Reflection Thought
A meaningful life is not built through control of outcomes, but through repeated alignment with who I choose to be.

A CLOSING LETTER TO THE READER

Dear Reader,

If you've made it this far, I want to say something clearly and sincerely:

I hope this book gave you relief.

Relief from carrying everything alone.
Relief from measuring yourself constantly.
Relief from believing that every moment is a test.

I hope it helped you see nothing is "wrong" with you for feeling pressure, doubt, fear or fatigue.

Those experiences don't mean you're weak.
They mean you're human and that you care.

My wish is not that you never struggle again.

It's that when you do, you remember this:

You don't have to abandon yourself in hard moments.
You don't have to rush to fix everything.
You don't have to wait until life settles to feel okay.

You can be present now.
You can choose your response now.
You can live aligned now.

And if some days all you manage is a small, honest response, that's enough.

That's the work.

Thank you for trusting these pages with something personal.

Wherever you are next, I hope you carry this with you:

You are allowed to strive without suffering.
You are allowed to care without carrying the weight.
You are allowed to live fully, right where you are.

Be Present.
Choose Well.
Repeat.

With Love, Gratitude & Respect,
Dan Armida

THE DAILY PRACTICE PAGE

A Simple Way to Live the Philosophy

You don't need a complicated routine.

You need a repeatable one.

Use this daily practice as a guide, not a rulebook.

MORNING (1–2 MINUTES)

Set the tone

What does today ask of me?

How do I want to show up?

What does "choosing well" look like today?

Quiet intention, not pressure.

IN THE MOMENT

When emotion rises

Notice what's happening

Take one breath

Ask: What response aligns with who I want to be?

Choose the next action

Presence first. Choice second.

AFTER DIFFICULT MOMENTS

Reset, don't replay

What can I learn?

What can I let go of?

What's the next honest step?

Keep the lesson. Release the weight.

EVENING (2–3 MINUTES)

Reflect, don't judge

Where was I present today?

Where did I choose well?

Where can I choose better tomorrow?

No scorekeeping. Just awareness.

THE REMINDER (ANYTIME)

When things feel heavy, return to this:

Be present with what's here.
Choose your response.
Let the outcome go.
Repeat.

FINAL NOTE ON THE PRACTICE

Some days this will feel easy.

Some days it will feel impossible.

Both are part of the practice.

You don't measure success by how calm you feel.

You measure it by how often you return.

And each return matters.